Fighting Back: Taekwondo for Women

YH Park and Jeff Leibowitz

With Color Photographs and Diagrams by

BuHo Choi

The Ultimate Reference Guide to Preventing Sexual Harassment, Assault and Rape

Table of Contents

Fighting Back: Taekwondo for Women
The Ultimate Reference Guide to Preventing Sexual Harassment, Assault and Rape

By YH Park and Jeff Leibowitz with Photographs and Diagrams by BuHo Choi

Cataloging Data

International Standard Book Number 9637151-1-9
Library of Congress Number 93-092768

THE WORLD TAEKWONDO FEDERATION

Recognized by the International Olympic Committee
Affiliated with the General Association of International Sports Federation

635 YUKSAMDONG, KANGNAMKU
SEOUL KOREA (135)
CABLE ADDRESS: WORLD TAEKWONDO

TELEPHONE: 82.2.5662505
82.2.557-5446
TELEX:K28870 WTFED
FACSIMILE: 82.2.553-4728

WTF President on:

Fighting Back: Taekwondo for Women

It is my great pleasure to welcome this new book on Taekwondo for Women. It comes at a time when society as a whole is coming to a new understanding of the rights of women and the need to protect them. The practice of taekwondo, while helpful in fostering the development of anyone, can be especially beneficial to women. Improved physical fitness, confidence, self-esteem, and the ability to defend yourself: all are benefits of taekwondo from which any woman can profit. I believe these benefits can help women to dictate the circumstances in which they choose to live and to live a freer, fuller and healthier life.

Taekwondo is the best means of self-defense. However, it is also an ancient art with strict ethical and moral stipulations. I was especially pleased, therefore, to note the authors' attempt to explain the many mental benefits that accompany training in its physical aspects. This work, while not intended to replace classroom instruction, is an invaluable asset, from which any woman interested in self-defense will benefit immensely.

This book is an important step. It addresses the special needs women require in today's society. I am delighted to give it my highest endorsement.

With Best Wishes to All,

Dr. Un Yong Kim, President
World Taekwondo Federation
Vice President,
International Olympic Committee

Preface

Taekwondo is a multifaceted art of which self-defense is only a small part. Taekwondo teaches people to strive for their best, physically and mentally. It has a rich heritage and its practitioners must adhere to strict ethical and moral guidelines. It is also a modern day Olympic sport. Yet it contains movements and modes of thought that clearly distinguish it as an art.

Thus the danger of writing a book that focuses on only one dimension of taekwondo--the risk of the reader wrongly inferring that taekwondo is merely a way of kicking and punching. The authors undertook this venture because it had been our feeling that the martial arts community and society in general needed a book that offered women solutions to the problems of sexual harassment, threats, assault and other violent crimes such as rape.

This book attempts to offer women practical solutions to these problems--virtually all of which are connected in some way to taekwondo. However, we have also attempted to illustrate that the practice of taekwondo, while effective for self-defense, is a lifelong venture into many paths of self-discovery. It is our hope that this book will be of use to practitioners and non-practitioners alike and that it will serve as a useful supplement to practice in any taekwondo school.

4

Introduction: Why Taekwondo for Self-Defense?

T his book was written in response to what the authors have felt to be a longstanding, legitimate demand. All of us face certain constraints in our lives, determined by a variety of things. Details as diverse as your location, mental alertness, type of friends, mode of dress and degree of assertiveness are all factors that determine the extent to which you may live free of societal and other constraints.

By constraints, we mean here things which hamper your ability to live your life as you see fit. Overcoming the--very justified--fear of sexual harassment, rape and other violent crimes that haunt many women is just one way to increase your freedom of thought and movement. However, learning to free yourself of the impediments that caused you to harbor these fears from the outset, is a far more reaching and valuable task. Taekwondo offers you the most effective means of self-defense possible. You will learn from this book that you have the potential to extricate yourself from virtually any type of confrontation. More importantly, though, you will find that you are capable of dictating the circumstances in which you live. Control, of yourself and those around you, is an essential part of your taekwondo training. Once you learn to stay in control of yourself, physically and mentally, you will have laid the groundwork needed to unearth your real potential, for a better body, a more focused and clear mind and a happier lifestyle.

Be forewarned, no one can "grant" you the benefits of taekwondo training. They come only as the result of hard training at a reputable school on a regular basis. Of one thing you can be certain: If you do make the decision to improve yourself with taekwondo, the rewards of your training will far exceed the demands. There are currently many books on the market claiming to provide "quick and easy" solutions to the problems posed by living in a society plagued as ours is with crimes of lurid natures. Learning the techniques provided in these manuals is, in fact, quick and easy. What is more difficult is applying them in situations where it counts. For instance, learning the vital parts of the anatomy where you can strike and disable an assailant is certainly important. But the often suggested notion that knowledge of where these areas lie combined with a basic understanding of how to use open hand techniques will engender fighting ability is completely erroneous. This assumption seeks to avoid one harsh reality: To defend yourself, you must practice seriously and on a regular basis. This book is an attempt to illustrate to women just how much power they have and how this power can be applied in self-defense situations. However, it is not the end-all of self-defense. Rather, it is an introduction to what you may expect to find in a taekwondo school. You will discover as you begin practicing the techniques contained herein that your as yet unused power exceeds the demands posed by societal dangers. As one example, women have far greater natural flexibility than men, and this will prove to be a valuable asset as you begin practice of taekwondo's powerful kicking techniques.

Proficiency in taekwondo will give you the ability, confidence and self-esteem you need to take charge of any situation. Once you make the decision to take control of your life, you will feel like a new, freer individual. The problems of living in a dangerous society will be of far less concern to you. You will therefore be able to focus on other concerns that will not only protect but enhance your well being. Thus the goal of this work: to grant you the option of fighting back, not just against crime, but the psychological effects of its presence. In the end, you will find that your abilities in self-defense are secondary to the psychological emancipation your study of taekwondo will bring about. The first step is to simply read this book and try out the techniques contained in it. Then, you may wish to enroll in a taekwondo school and further explore the possibilities described. The choice, as you shall see, is yours.

-1-
Taekwondo: More than Just Self-Defense

S ince its Olympic debut in 1988, taekwondo's popularity has spread like wildfire across the world. People of all ages and walks of life have taken up this ancient Korean martial art and modern day sport to improve themselves in a variety of ways. Better stamina, endurance, physical fitness, mental

Taekwondo has achieved great success with the American public, partly because of its adaptability. Anyone can do taekwondo and students from all walks of life and all ages are practicing this ancient art and Olympic sport.

acuity, and the ability to defend themselves with incredible speed and power: all result from diligent taekwondo training.

But why should taekwondo prevail as your choice for self-defense? Because self-defense, for better or worse, requires continual practice. There is an adage that has it that people react the way they train. If you do not train at all, you will be unable to defend yourself should the need arise. And training in

Taekwondo can help you achieve mastery over yourself as well as the circumstances in which you live. But it requires diligent practice at a reputable school on a regular basis. There are no "quick and easy" solutions to the problems of self-defense posed in today's society.

taekwondo gives you ample reason to practice; as you refine your physical abilities, you will find yourself improving in many other areas in which you probably had expressed no interest. A relaxed state of mind, improved patience, better concentrative powers and numerous other benefits will accompany your new self-defense skills.

Seventy percent of the techniques used in taekwondo are kicks. A kick is far more powerful than a punch, and if learned properly, just as easy to

About 70% of the techniques used in taekwondo are kicks.
Taekwondo relies primarily on kicks because of their
explosive power as compared to punches.

Your leg is much longer than the arm of the average assailant. This reach advantage is a great asset in a self-defense situation and can help you to blunt an attack before it gets close enough to pose real danger.

throw. Your legs also are much longer than your arms. If you can kick well, you can hit your attacker before he gets close enough to touch you. You may have noticed that women are naturally far more flexible than men. Taekwondo will teach you to put this flexibility to good use. You will learn to end a potentially dangerous situation before an attacker can make it materialize. If, however, an assailant does get past your kicking range, your arsenal will by no

means be depleted. Hand strikes, wrist throws and other take-downs are just some ways to deal with an attacker in close. Moreover, if you are earnest in your training, you will find after a few months that's it's not so easy to get past your kicking range. You can use your natural flexibility to mete-out serious blows from in close. You will then only resort to hand techniques on rare occasion.

To prepare for the kicks you'll need, you'll first need to warm up and then stretch. You should always

With regular practice, you will find that your kicks are just as formidable at close range as when they are thrown from a distance.

do this before any physical activity and especially one as demanding on the legs as taekwondo. As you begin practice, you will find that your flexibility will increase fairly drastically after the first few months. From about the fourth month to the twelfth, your improvement will come at a slower rate. However, after about six months you will acquire sufficient skill

Women are naturally far more flexible than men. This will be a great advantage as you undertake your study of taekwondo. In taekwondo, people are taught to use their natural assets, as well as those they have not yet discovered. You are probably far more flexible than you think.

to trounce an unarmed assailant. Improved flexibility will not only make your kicks faster and more powerful--it will also improve blood flow, endurance, speed, and the rate at which you heal. As a result, virtually any physical activity will be easier. The following five exercises will help you to begin warming-up and stretching.:

Modified Squats: Standing up with your hands pointed straight, swing your arms down and behind as you bend your knees into a squat at the same time. Stand as you swing your hands back up. Repeat this ten times.

Arm Swings: From the same position, swing both arms to the left, middle, front, then behind and back to the starting position. Repeat this five times on both sides.

Down and Back: Spread your legs double shoulder width and bring both hands down to the floor in front of you. Next, touch them under your legs. Rise up slow, brace your back, lean, then return to the

Taekwondo practitioners use special warm-up exercises to prepare themselves for the rigor of kicking practice. Modified squats are an excellent way to begin warming up.

original position. Stay in each position only momentarily, and try to maintain a steady rhythm--be careful not to bounce though. Bouncing only <u>reduces</u> flexibility by making muscles contract more than they stretch: Relax, take your time and get the most from each movement.

Trunk Twist From the same leg position, let your arms dangle in front of you. Swing them around to each side, then to the back and front while swiveling

You should always warm up before stretching. You will be doing lots of kicks and must warm and loosen as many muscles as possible. The arm swing is one way to loosen your upper body muscles.

17

As you perform the "down and back" exercise, you will loosen your leg, lower back and abdominal muscles.

your hips. As you go toward each direction (the front, sides and back) let gravity and the weight of your arms help you reach as far as possible. Move slowly and control your breathing. Some beginners have a tendency to hold their breath when experiencing physical stress, for instance while doing a difficult exercise like push-ups. As a general rule, exhale during the hard part of an exercise, like the "up" part

18

Windmills are an easy yet efficient exercise that will prepare your body for the rigor of taekwondo.

of a push-up and inhale during the easier "down" side. Learning to control your breathing is an important first step in learning control of your body.

Windmills Windmills are a relatively simple exercise with which most people are familiar. From the same leg position, bring your right hand to your left leg, then your left to your right, alternating sides as quickly as possible. Try to keep your arms straight. Imagining that there is a five foot piece of wood taped to the back of your arms is a good way to practice; it will help you to get the most from the exercise by providing a greater range of motion to it.

Whether warming up or practicing hard, be sure to breathe out when there is stress on your heart, for instance on the "up" part of a push up or when extending a punch.

*If you stretch regularly, you will kick with power and speed.
You also will find that virtually any physical activity requires
less effort.*

-2-
The Targets

O nce you're warmed up and stretched, you're ready to practice basic strikes. While the following kicks can wreak havoc on an attacker, note well: They are useless in and of themselves. You must not only know how to throw a kick, but where and when. Timing, stepping, determining how much force is commensurate with the degree of danger present--all are necessary to put

your kicks to good use. However, you should also know that no reputable instructor will teach you these kicks as distinct from taekwondo stances and footwork. To ensure that your kicks are thrown from the right position, you'll first need to learn a basic fighting stance.

To do this, you must learn to make and use a fist. Your fist should always make contact with the two big knuckles. These are the first two from the left on

When you make a fist, be sure to wrap your thumb around the front of the two fingers next to it. Also, be sure to strike with your two big knuckles. This will help you land focused, powerful blows.

23

your right hand and the first two from the right on your left. If you strike with the other, smaller knuckles, you risk serious injury, thereby jeopardizing your physical well-being when you need it most. Be sure that your thumb wraps around the two fingers next to it. Your wrist should point straight or slightly down to help the knuckles protrude.

Now, assume a basic fighting stance (*"Kyroogi Ja Say"* in Korean) by placing your legs shoulder width

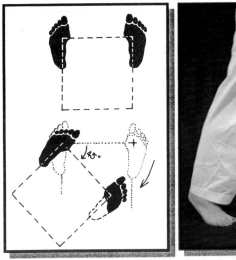 

Your fighting stance should feel comfortable and natural. Keep your legs one shoulder width apart, not wider. Too much distance between your legs will inhibit movement and waste time you might otherwise use to throw a strike.

24

apart, then taking a step back. Step as you would naturally, otherwise you'll wind up in a stance that is too wide or narrow (there are dangerous pitfalls to each). As you put your hands up, be sure that the lead hand is at about eye level with the rear hand a bit lower. The arm of the rear hand should be in front of and thus protecting your solar plexus. If you've ever had the wind knocked out of you, you'll know where your solar plexus is--at the spot above your stomach

The solar plexus is a primary target in taekwondo. A solid blow to an attacker's solar plexus should knock the wind out of him and buy you the time needed for escape.

but below your chest.

Always dance lightly on the balls of your feet when in a fighting stance and keep your weight distributed evenly. The long, deep stances you see in movies have no place in reality. If you put too much weight on one leg, you will first have to shift it to the other before you can kick. This shifting wastes precious seconds which should be used to strike. If you keep your weight evenly distributed, you should feel comfortable and light footed, able to move any direction any time with no discomfort. To learn kicks,

26

you must first understand where they should be directed. The following is a description--from the bottom up--of the primary targets to which you should aim your techniques:

The Instep: Your instep is composed of many small bones, all of which can easily be broken. Moreover, it is sensitive to direct strikes; imagine, for instance, the stomp of a high heeled shoe on your instep.

A solid blow to the instep can incapacitate virtually any assailant. Remember, though, when you throw any strike, you are making a commitment to fight instead of flee. You must therefore strike with as much force as possible.

The Shin: The shin is another highly sensitive area, the main advantage of which is that it is often exposed. As an example, if you were being grabbed from behind, the shin--and instep--of the assailant are vulnerable to your downward stomp. Or, just imagine the fighting stances you may have seen before; no one keeps their guard down by their shins.

The Knee: Many people consider knees strong parts of their body able to withstand forceful impact. This

The knee is an excellent target. You can strike it with a Roundhouse Kick, which will buckle your opponent, or straight in with a Side Kick, which is more effective and will cause serious damage if done properly.

A solid blow to the knee can save the day in a self-defense situation. Strikes such as these should of course be thrown with caution. When you have decided that your safety is in jeopardy, though, you should throw knee strikes with no hesitation whatsoever.

is hardly the case as anyone with knee trouble will attest. A proper strike to the knee will buckle your opponent and give you time to decide whether additional blows are necessary.

The Groin: One of the difficult points to make to anyone learning self-defense is that when safety is compromised the rules of "fair play" get tossed. When your life is at stake there are no rules. You must take any action needed to free yourself from danger. A strike to the groin can save the day in a self-defense

situation. You should have no hesitation in using such a strike should the circumstance dictate.

The Ribs: The ribs are excellent targets. Note, however, that the lower two ribs are far weaker than those above them. If you throw a solid strike to the lower ribs, your opponent will likely keel over, and they will probably break. Should you hit the upper ribs, you will probably knock your opponent back but

Blows to the side should be directed to the lower ribs. These are floating and break much easier than those above them. As always, try to put your weight into your strikes and focus on your target area. If you do this, you should break your assailants lower two ribs and buy the time you need to get to safety.

31

A focused strike to the solar plexus will knock the wind out of your attacker, granting you the time you need to decide whether follow up techniques are called for.

without inflicting damage. There may of course be times when the latter option is preferable. However, when you need to escape serious danger, a blow to the lower ribs will better facilitate your escape.

The Solar Plexus: As you know, the solar plexus is just above your ribs and below your stomach. A solid blow there will knock the wind out of your attacker, buying you time to flee.

The Sternum: Your sternum is comprised of bone and cartilage. It is located where your ribs meet at the point above your solar plexus. A powerful blow to

A strike to the front or side of the neck can be a formidable blow if delivered with proper technique. The neck is an excellent target area and is often attacked after a strike that has keeled an attacker over, such as one to the groin.

the sternum can cause serious damage, and as with all strikes, should be executed with discretion.

The Neck: Both the throat and the sides of the neck are primary targets which can be struck to quickly incapacitate an assailant. A good kick to the neck will put an end to any self-defense situation.

The Chin: A blow to the chin--thrown up, across or straight at it--can cause serious damage to the jaw and teeth. Some strikes, such as the uppercut, are thrown almost exclusively at the chin.

The Nose: A strong blow to the nose can separate the cartilage there from the bone. Contrary to popular belief, you cannot "break" someone's nose. If you have ever seen a skull, you may have noticed that there is simply a cavity in the area the nose was. However, a good shot in the nose is obviously quite painful and can put a quick end to a confrontation.

The Eyes: A strike to the eye such as a straight punch, Backfist or Spearfinger is useful in that it can temporarily--or even permanently--blind an assailant and grant you the time needed to make haste.

A strike to the chin can wreak havoc on an attacker, damaging the jaw as well as the teeth and lips.

The Temple: The temple is the point directly behind your eyes on the front portion of the side of your head. A blow to the temple can leave your attacker in an impaired, almost drunken state. This will reduce the threat and put you in a far better position for negotiation or escape.

The above is by no means an exhaustive list. Rather, it is designed to give you general ideas as to the targets you should think about as you begin

A concentrated attack to the eyes can blind your assailant. A good Backfist to to the head can put him in a semi-conscious state. When you strike, you must focus on your target area.

As you train and progress in taekwondo, you will find that
you can deliver a kick as easily as a punch.

36

practicing strikes. As your kicks become more formidable, you will find that you do not need a hundred percent accuracy. If, for instance, you develop a powerful Side Kick and aim it at your attacker's neck but inadvertently strike his face or stomach, the result as far as your escape is concerned is bound to be the same. As you improve, you will nevertheless learn to throw your strikes with

It is important that you make contact when practicing, preferably with another person. If that is not possible, however a heavy bag or striking pads can be helpful in learning to isolate and strike vulnerable target areas.

*As your techniques become more and more powerful, you
will find that you can throw them to virtually any target
area with relative ease.*

38

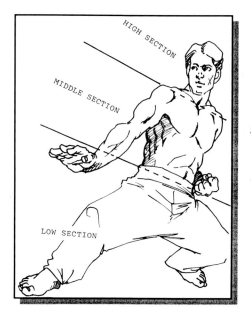

It is helpful to think of your target areas as being divided among three sections: low, middle and high.

increased accuracy and control--over the force, height, snap, thrust and every other aspect of a kick. But you will find that your kicks will pack so much power that you really won't worry much about the exact point of impact. Instead, you'll probably start thinking in terms of three sections: low, middle and high. The low section is that below the waist; the middle is that from the waist to the upper chest and the high section is the neck on up.

Once you've gleaned a general understanding of the primary target areas, you're ready to learn the kicks of taekwondo. Every kick is different, and you should strive to improve their form from the outset. With time and practice, you will develop an intuitive sense as to when it is appropriate to throw which kick. If you kick incorrectly,

Knowing when to throw a kick is just as important as knowing how to throw the kick itself. You will learn timing only as a result of of training on a regular basis.

Taekwondo practitioners have a vast arsenal of techniques from which they may draw. You must adapt your techniques so they are appropriate for the situation.

however, you risk not only missing the chance to land a blow, but of injuring yourself. By working to improve your form, by practicing your kicks on a regular, ideally daily basis, you will develop a vast and varied arsenal that can be used to defeat attackers physically much stronger than yourself.

The first kick you'll need is the Front Snap Kick or *"Ahp Chagi"* in Korean. Like many kicks it is best to learn the Front Snap Kick in four parts: up, out, back and down. To begin practice, start from your fighting stance. Remember, your feet should be spread shoulder length and width, and you must dance lightly on the balls of your feet. You should feel comfortable and relaxed. If you are tense, you'll not only slow your techniques but you'll be more apt to make unnecessary reactions as well.

It is important that--almost--all kicks be thrown off your rear leg. It should not matter which leg you

A kick thrown off the rear leg is vastly superior to one thrown off the front. A rear-leg kick allows you to put full force behind a kick. However, a rear leg kick is also a bit slower than a front leg kick. You must thus throw your kicks with total confidence and proper timing. Believing in your abilities is extremely important in taekwondo. If you have confidence, it will be clearly evident--- in your techniques and your overall attitude.

The Front Snap Kick or "Ahp Chagi" is an extremely simple yet effective technique which relies heavily on the leg's quick snapping motion. Be sure to curl your toes back and strike with the ball of your foot.

43

Your front snap kick must shoot out from a chamber. If it is not chambered, you will be unable to generate the snap upon which the kick relies.

put back, however, because you must kick equally well with each. For simplicity's sake, however, begin with your right side back. Your right leg is therefore your kicking leg. As you lift this leg into the first chamber, be sure to raise your rear hand a little. As you kick, your body is turning more forward than it had been in the fighting stance. As a result, the part of your face that had been behind is now facing front and must be protected. You can accomplish this fairly easily by raising your rear hand. Now snap the kick straight out, curling back your toes to expose and hit with the ball of your foot. Next, immediately snap the kick back to the spot from which it left, then touch down. When you begin practicing this kick in sparring class, you will see that there are many advantages to landing forward after you kick. In the meantime, though, it is better to land back and concentrate on developing good form.

The Roundhouse Kick, or *"Dolryo Chagi"* is easily the most popular technique in taekwondo. One reason is that it can be thrown quickly in diverse situations. Unlike the Front Snap Kick, the Roundhouse Kick makes contact with the instep. You

should thus point your toes straight to avoid injuring them. To practice, begin from a fighting stance with your right side back. Bring your right leg up and around as if your were lifting it over a chair as you kick. Turn your hips into the kick as you snap it out, back and then touch down. As your leg reaches full extension, it is important that it be aligned with the side of your body. Do not bend your upper body as you throw the Roundhouse Kick. This error is common among beginners, and it important to avoid

Like the Front Snap Kick, it is important that the Roundhouse Kick or "Dolyro Chagi" be launched from a proper chamber. Turn your hips as much as possible into your Roundhouse Kick and strike with the instep.

46

One way to help improve the form of your Roundhouse Kick is by practicing with a chair or similar object. Place the chair next to you and make sure your first chamber rides up above it. This will help ensure that you chamber your kicks fully.

it from the start as it offsets your stability and decreases power. A good Roundhouse Kick combines snap with thrust and can thus land with speed and power. Although the kick ranks high among many enthusiasts because of its speed, a Roundhouse Kick to the knee, groin, solar plexus, neck or head can easily incapacitate the average, or even above average assailant.

The Side Kick or *Yop Chagi* is a bit slower than the Roundhouse Kick. It is an excellent linear strike that works especially well in self-defense situations where it can be applied to the shin, knee, groin, throat or face. Developing a good Side Kick can be an arduous, time-consuming process requiring regular practice and much patience. The Side Kick is one of the more difficult kicks to teach because it is very different from, yet often confused with the Roundhouse Kick. You should take care to distinguish them from the start.

*A good Side Kick or "Yop Chagi" can take some time to develop. **Do not confuse it with a roundhouse kick.** Unlike the Roundhouse, the Side Kick shoots straight from a chamber. To make this chamber, **it is imperative that you turn your hips.** Then shoot the leg straight out and hit with the heel.*

To practice the Side Kick, assume a fighting stance with your right side back. Bring your right knee as close as possible to your left chest without hunching over. While in this position be sure that your heel protrudes and that your toes point horizontally, not downward. Now shoot the kick straight out, return it to its original chamber, then put it down. As you bring the kick up to its original chamber, pivot your body, swiveling on your

Wrong   *Right*

When you throw a sidekick you keep your ribs in a straight line with your leg (when it is fully extended). If you do, your kick will pack tremendous power. If not, you risk serious injury.

Even if you can throw a picture perfect side kick, you must keep your hands up---whenever you kick. Bear in mind: The best time to kick someone is when they themselves are throwing a kick. Think of your body as a unit in which the movement of one part affects the whole. You must not forget your upper body when throwing kicks, nor your lower body when punching. All are connected, and your training will help you to think of them as such.

supporting leg. As you do this you will again need to adjust your guard. This is especially important with the Side Kick, given that you are turning your body 180 degrees, thus exposing what had been the rear part of your face. To change guard, simply bring the hand that had been behind toward the front of your face when your body is turned and your face exposed.

Return your guard to its original position after completing the kick.

It can take a great deal of time to develop the flexibility, coordination and timing needed to throw a good side kick at any height. However, even in the beginning, it is still an excellent weapon for self-defense if thrown low, to the shin, knee or groin. As you become more proficient in your kicking skills you will find that kicking head height does not require a great deal more exertion than kicking low. But as you refine your skills, it is advisable to practice all of your kicks to the low section. This way, you are more likely to kick properly because you will not compromise form due to inflexibility. Further, at the initial stages of your training, you will find that it is easier to kick low than high. This will provide you with a viable means of self-defense while allowing you to concentrate on developing more advanced skills.

If you can throw kicks head height in training, landing one to the knee or other lower body parts will come quite easy.

Women have far greater natural flexibility than men. This is an asset you can exploit by developing kicking proficiency. One way to give this notion practical application is by practicing the Axe Kick, or *"Nerie Chigi"*. The Axe Kick does not have chambers as do the previously described kicks. Even if you are relatively new to taekwondo, this is one of the few kicks that works to the high section at the incipient stages of your training.

The Axe Kick or "Nerie Chigi" swings up above the opponent's head, and then downward on his face or chest.

To practice the Axe Kick, assume a fighting stance with your right side back. Now swing your rear (right) leg up as high as you can as you let your rear foot slide forward. The kick strikes on its way down. Ideally, you should make contact with the heel, which should land on your assailant's face after having risen well above it. If this seems impossible, remember that you have a vast reservoir of as yet unused physical abilities. Without trying, you will never discover them; with regular practice, however, your axe kick

will become second nature, and kicking head height will not seem like an astounding feat at all. When throwing your axe kick, bend the leg slightly as it rises up. Then, snap it as it swings down. By combining the kick's downward swing with snap, your axe kick will be a devastating technique for which few attackers will be prepared.

-4-
Hand Strikes

Although taekwondo practitioners favor kicking techniques because they are more powerful than punches, there is no escaping the fact that hands play a role in almost any self-defense situation you'll encounter before becoming highly proficient. In addition to the aforementioned kicks, you will thus need to understand some basic hand strikes. Start from your fighting stance with

In certain instances, hand strikes could be your only option. As with your kicks, you must practice them so they become instinctual when it counts.

57

Punches thrown off of your rear hand pack far more force than those thrown off your front.

your right side back. As you'll recall, your hands are up in fists with the forward hand at about eye level and the rear hand near your solar plexus. Remember, kicks are more powerful when thrown off the rear leg. The same concept applies to punches. A punch thrown off your rear hand will pack much more power than one off of your forward hand. You can, however, use your forward hand for a variety of reasons, one of which is to set up a more powerful strike off your rear hand. The Jab-Punch (*"Ahp Chirugi"*) is an excellent front hand strike, which relies heavily on a good snap. Thrown to the face, it will not only inflict damage as a result of its speed but will set up your attacker for another, more powerful punch, to the face, solar plexus or ribs. The Jab Punch is easily thrown from your fighting stance because your forward hand is already in a fist, not just protecting your face, but ready to launch a lead hand strike. From your fighting stance, the knuckles of your forward hand are pointed upward. When you land a Jab Punch, your knuckles must be horizontal.

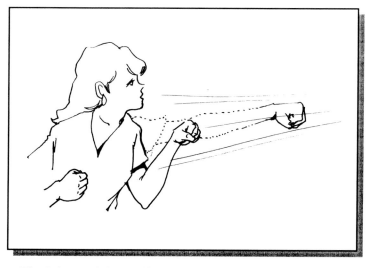

The Jab Punch is an effective way to set up a more powerful strike off your rear hand.

Timed properly, the Jab Punch can itself be a very effective technique. Remember, the best time to strike someone is when they themselves are attempting a strike.

Therefore, when you throw a Jab Punch, it is essential that you twist your punching hand. You will find that this twisting motion plays an important role in many of the blocks and punches you'll learn, even at the very advanced level. The twist also gives your punch more snap and power. After impact, the punch should immediately retract to the spot from which it left, ready to be pumped out again. If you do not return it to its starting point, you risk exposing your face and head to a counter-attack that could include any of a

One way to make sure your elbow remains behind your Jab Punch is to practice next to a wall. If your elbow touches the wall, it is a signal that you are throwing it incorrectly.

number of things. As you pump out the jab, be sure not to let your elbow slide out to the side. One effective way to ensure this is to practice your Jab Punch standing astride a wall. If your elbow is not directly behind your punch, your arm will touch the wall--a signal from which you should take heed. It is important that your Jab-Punch shoot-out straight, not in a circular motion. The shortest distance between two points is a straight line. A straight punch is therefore faster than a circular one. There are of course circular strikes such as the hook punch, which can also be thrown off the forward hand. But when throwing a linear strike such as the Jab-Punch it is important that there be no confusion between straight and circular strikes. After you feel comfortable with the Jab-Punch, throw it at something such as a heavy bag, focus pad or willing partner to acquaint yourself with the feeling of impact. Turn your shoulders. This will put the force of your body weight behind the strike. If you do not put your weight behind the strike, you risk throwing a weak punch with only the

The Jab Punch works well on a number of target areas, among them the jaw.

power of your arm behind it. The difference in power between a good punch and an arm punch is substantial. Always put your body weight behind your punches.

One problem many women have when it comes to learning self-defense is that they have had much less exposure to contact sports and impact in general than men. If they are struck, they often feel traumatized and this fear makes them vulnerable to further attack.

Wrong   *Right*

As with all strikes, it is important that you put your body weight into your jab punch.

It is important that you occasionally absorb a strike (while wearing full safety gear). This will help you to remain calm and to react more effectively should you be struck outside of your taekwondo school. Often, women who have never experienced contact, freeze up in a self-defense situation because they are traumatized by having been struck. Desensitizing yourself to this is one step toward putting yourself on equal footing with your assailant.

By training on a regular basis, you will not only de-sensitize yourself to making contact, but to absorbing it as well. You will learn that if you are faced with a serious self-defense problem and have been struck that you are able to remain calm, assess the situation systematically and determine the most plausible means of escape. No one enjoys being struck and training in

By training in a taekwondo, you will learn to remain calm and react appropriately in a street encounter.

taekwondo will certainly not make the prospect more appealing. What it will do is alert you to the fact that you are capable of throwing fast and powerful strikes, of learning to control your body and of thereby having greater control over the circumstances around you. You will also discover that your fear of pain was disproportionate to that which the average assailant is able to inflict.

The Backfist or *"Dung Chumuck Chigi"* is similar to the Jab-Punch, although it is more commonly thrown to the side of the head while the

Jab Punch is usually directed at frontal targets, such as the face or neck. Start from your fighting stance with your right side back, making your right your lead hand. Now, pretend there is someone in front of you in a stance like yours. If you were to extend your forward hand, you would see that you can reach the back of your fist to the side of your opponent's temple even if his hands are up. The Backfist can thus be a somewhat deceptive technique because it

The Backfist or "Dung Chumuck Chigi" is another lead hand strike that is useful for setting up more powerful strikes off of your rear hand.

If your opponent tries to block your Backfist, all the better.
Use the opportunity to slam in a rear hand strike to his
(now exposed) lower ribs.

can sneak around an opponent's defenses. If you land the Backfist with good snap and form, you can easily put your opponent into a daze. But even if the technique fails, it can still help you out of a bind because your assailant may try to block it with his forward hand. Once he does, he exposes his ribs. You can now take advantage of the opening to slam in a more powerful rear-hand punch.

When throwing a Backfist, it is important that you resist the natural temptation to first wind up by bringing your striking hand back before throwing it forward. Many beginners unwittingly wind up their Backfist. Practicing in front of a mirror can help avoid or correct this error. The difficulty with winding up the strike is that it *telegraphs* to your opponent what technique you are about to throw.

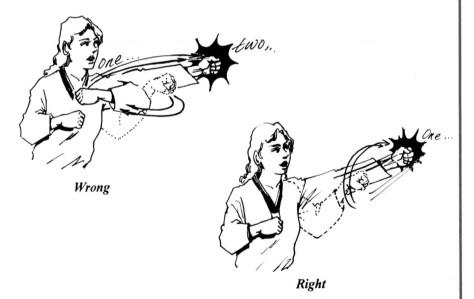

Wrong

Right

Do not wind up your Backfist. Shoot it straight out from its original starting point. Otherwise your opponent will be wise to what you are doing and will have a chance to take defensive measures.

This gives him time to react to your strike, which can lead to disaster. The Backfist is not only deceiving in the way it snakes around an opponent's defenses, it is also deceptively fast. A good Backfist can put an immediate end to a confrontation. And if you are not yet proficient and wind up telegraphing, you will nevertheless set-up your opponent for a Reverse Punch to the lower ribs.

The Reverse Punch, called *"Twi Choomuk" is* among the most powerful hand strikes in taekwondo. It is always thrown off the rear hand and is thus a more forceful strike than the Backfist. When used in conjunction, however, the Jab Punch can lead the way for the more powerful Reverse Punch. To practice your Reverse Punch alone, start from your fighting stance, dancing lightly on the balls of your feet. Now pretend there is a rope tied around your rear hand with the other end tied to a truck. The truck is revving up, getting ready to pull away with lightening speed. As the truck bolts forward your hand shoots straight out and your upper body turns. The turn of your body is especially important with the Reverse Punch, given that it relies on a combination of speed, power, proper form and commitment. All are tied in to a proper turn. As you know, the correct striking area for any punch is your two big knuckles. Bear this in mind when you do your Jab or Reverse Punch. You will definitely feel a difference when you begin

The Reverse Punch or "Twi Choomuck" is among the most common hand strikes in taekwondo. By combining speed with power, your reverse punch can both surprise and disable an assailant.

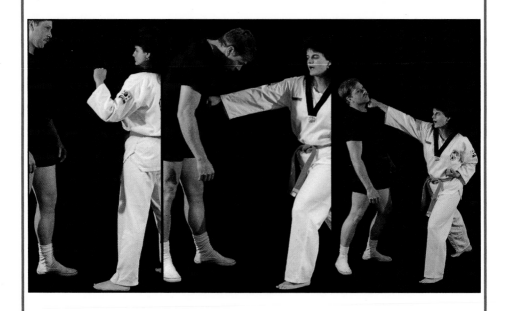

After throwing a reverse punch, it is important that you return your hand to its starting position so you are prepared to strike again.

practicing your strikes with a heavy bag or partner. Visualizing the truck pulling your hand is an effective way to conceptualize the launching of a reverse Punch. However, you must snap the punch back to its original starting point after making contact and to be ready to let rip with one or more follow-up punches.

-5-
Taking Charge, Kick-Punch Combinations

B eing able to throw a strike with speed and power will result only from diligent training. If, however, you are unable to put your strikes together into fluid combinations, you risk creating an all or nothing scenario in a self-defense encounter. This severely limits your options and decreases the

By learning combinations, you will be able to overwhelm your opponent with a blitz of techniques. You will also free yourself from the burden of relying on only one technique at a time and the "all or nothing" scenario this creates.

73

You should not think of your combinations as having distinct movements. Rather, think of the combination as a unit in itself. This will help you in not wasting time in between strikes. Here a Roundhouse Kick is immediately followed up with an Axe Kick.

likelihood of escape. One way to avoid the pitfalls of throwing only single strikes is to practice and think of certain techniques as joined. Many beginners concentrate so hard when throwing a Front Snap Kick, for instance, that they forget their hands altogether. If it were to miss they will have landed with their hands down, in an extremely vulnerable position. One way to compensate for this is to

Combinations must flow smoothly. One way to ensure this is begin a strike before the preceding one is finished. Here the Jab Punch is readied before the Front Snap Kick has landed.

occasionally practice your Front Snap Kick as if it were connected to your Jab Punch. Your combinations must flow smoothly, and you needn't wait for one technique to finish before throwing the next. In any kick-punch combination, you must prepare the punch *as you are kicking*.

To try this, start from your fighting stance, dancing lightly on the balls of your feet with your right side back. As always, it is better to practice with a partner holding a focus pad as opposed to kicking only air. If no one is available or if you do not yet have a focus pad, it is nevertheless worthwhile to practice your strikes with no tangible target. Unlike before, where you were practicing only a single strike at a time so as to concentrate on learning proper form, it is essential that you now *land forward* after throwing the Front Snap Kick. As you kick, remember to switch your hands; the right hand that was behind is now in front and therefore higher than

When you are practicing the Front Snap Kick to improve its form, you may land the kick back to its original position after you extend it. When throwing combinations, however, you will need to land forward to prepare for the next technique.

76

It is crucial that you switch your guard as you kick.
Otherwise, your head is vulnerable to attack.

your left, which is now the rear hand. However, you should unleash the Jab the moment after the Front Snap Kick makes contact and before your foot has landed. With a good snap, there is no reason to waste precious seconds waiting for the kick to touch ground before striking. Snap it out. As it snaps back, land forward with your Jab Punch. Ideally, the kick should be aimed at the attacker's groin and the punch to the throat. Other areas, such as the eyes or temple may also be targeted.

The Front Snap Kick and Jab Punch are quick, reliable techniques, which are effective after relatively little practice. They are therefore particularly useful for confrontations in which you feel you must react lest your adversary do so first. In a self-defense encounter, the person who throws the first strike is at a definite advantage. You must be sure that this person is you. If you feel threatened, you can

If you feel threatened, you should unleash the first strike--as quickly and forcefully as you can. Allowing your attacker to get in the first strike can put you at a serious disadvantage.

78

If, after throwing a strike you feel a follow up is needed, you must do so before you assailant has time to regain his composure. Here, after delivering a front snap kick, the defender follows up with a forearm to the head. Once you have incapacitated an attacker, you should flee the scene as soon as possible and notify the police.

unleash a Front Snap Kick followed with a Jab Punch off your forward hand in under two seconds. You can then use the time your potential assailant's pain buys to escape. The Front Snap Kick can be followed with a variety of other open or closed hand techniques, with which you should be acquainted. One is the Forearm Strike or *Palgup Chigi*. Although it is not technically part of your hand, the forearm and elbow are usually referred to as hand strikes, simply to distinguish them from kicks.

A proper Forearm Strike can cause serious damage, especially if thrown to the temple or face with proper timing. To practice, assume a fighting stance with your right side back. This time, as you throw your Front Snap Kick, land forward with your Forearm Strike instead of the Jab Punch. The blow

A forearm strike packs formidable power and, if focused properly, can put an abrupt halt to an attacker's plans.

As you throw your initial attack, keep an eye open for what will be the best follow-up. This requires split second decision making, which you will cultivate as you train in taekwondo.

should land square against your potential assailant's head, ideally hitting his temple. As with the Front Snap Kick, you will get more power from your hand strike because your weight comes forward. You can channel this incoming power into your hand strikes. Note that if you were to follow through with this strike, you could then reverse motion and slam in an elbow from the opposite direction.

A Front Snap Kick followed up with a two fingered eye attack can help you escape an impending attack. Be sure to snap out your strikes--one immediately following the other, and be ready for further follow ups, should the situation warrant.

Next try following your Front Snap Kick with an upward Elbow Strike. To do this, simply lift up your elbow with a quick snap. Thrown to the chin, this strike can leave your attacker incapacitated. As before, begin your strike before your kicking leg has touched down. The next strike you should try is a Two Fingered Eye Attack. This too can be practiced as an immediate follow up to a Front Snap Kick. Unlike the other strikes, however, you will have to open your striking hand. Do this once the kick makes contact. After you slash the kick out and snap in the strike--with the two fingers next to your thumb each striking one eye--return your hand to a fist. Standing in a self-defense situation with your hands open can be perilous as your fingers are susceptible to damage from an opponent's strikes.

Your kick must be launched before your attacker gets past your kicking range. Remember, your legs are longer than his hands. If you use them properly, you can cut off his attack before it begins. Once your attacker gets a hold of you, you are in a whole new ball game, which we shall discuss in the next chapter. In the meantime, try putting together as many combinations as possible with the techniques you've learned. This will help you to react forcefully and with confidence the moment you need to. And this is *before* the assailant has had sufficient time to get hold of you.

It is important that you strike your attacker before he has a chance to get a hold of you. Otherwise you risk his landing one or more blows thus jeopardizing you chances of escape.

85

-6-
Escaping Holds

What if an attacker gets past your defenses and does get a hold of you? Contrary to popular belief, and probably your own instincts, your options are not nearly as limited as you might think. A basic understanding of how to position your legs when in close, your knowledge of primary targets combined with that of basic kicking and striking techniques will give you a definitive

Escaping from holds such as these are fairly simple. You should thus not let fear dictate how you react.

upper hand.

The first hold you will need to defend against is a *rear arm lock*. Assume your attacker is holding your right arm behind your back with his right hand. First, step back with your left leg and use your body weight to slam in a left elbow to his left temple. Take a step forward with your left leg and grab his right hand with your right. Next, step back one step (clockwise) with your right leg as you use your grasp to help swing your attacker around. Your attacker is now open to your Front Snap Kick. Snap it into his

When you react to any hold, you must do so swiftly, before your attacker has a chance to tighten his grip.

 solar plexus. Having been slammed in the head and solar plexus, your assailant should by now be weakened if not unconscious. However, people who involve themselves with alcohol or illicit drugs often have resilience beyond their natural physical means. If this is the case and your attacker is still aggressive, step your right leg well behind his, keeping it bent. This should be fairly easy since you have just kicked and landed forward, near his right leg. As you do this, grab his throat. Now, use your grasp of his throat to pull him over your leg. To facilitate the throw, straighten out your bent leg as you pull him over in a circular motion. You will find that this snap, combined with your grasp and the fact that your attacker is already destabilized, all contribute to his landing with a resounding thud. Now is the time to escape the scene.

1

Step back and slam
in an elbow.

2

Step forward with
your left leg.

3

Step back with your right
leg and retain your grasp
of his arm.

4

Slash your kick into
your attacker's solar
plexus.

89

Another common grab is the *rear choke*. You should take care in learning the stepping motion used to defend against this attack as it is useful in defending against several other types of assaults. The idea is to move your legs so as to make a big letter "C". To understand this motion, simply stand facing front with your feet in a natural position. Bring your left foot to your right in a clockwise circular motion, then back in the same direction so as to form the "C". Now have someone grab you in a rear choke using their right hand. As you apply this step, you will notice that you are first stepping toward your attacker's arm, then landing behind him. As you do this, slam in a left elbow to your attacker's face. He should now be falling over your left leg in a circular motion with his groin exposed. As he falls over your left leg, slam in a Bottomfist with your right hand. A Bottomfist is a downward strike, using a fist, that hits with the side of your hand nearest your little finger. This should send your attacker reeling. It should also leave him unable to get up to pursue further

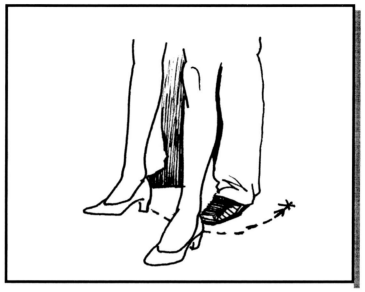

The "C" step is an important motion that can help you turn the table on an attacker in a variety of self-defense situations.

advances. Use this time to flee. Another grab you'll need to learn to defend against is the *bear hug*. Here again your ability to do the "C" step may be decisive. There are two basic types of bear hugs--one that traps your arms and one that does not. For the one in which your arms are free, you may try a reaction that is very similar to that used to escape a rear choke. Simply make the "C" step the moment you feel the assailant's arms take hold. Follow up with the same elbow

1

To escape the rear choice, make a "C" step.

To escape the rear choice, make a "C" step.

2

Slam in a left elbow as your attacker starts to fall over.

3

Throw a bottomfist to the groin.

4

Flee the scene as fast as possible.

strike and Bottomfist as you did with the rear choke escape. A bear hug in which your attacker has your arms trapped would seem to pose a greater problem. Remember, however, your attacker is tying up both of his arms with his hold. Although uncomfortable, your situation is by no means inescapable. First, slam the back of your head into his face. Second, stomp on his instep with your heel. Third, lift your stomping leg straight up into his groin. Now, use your "C" step,

Escaping a bear hug is a simple. More important than the physical techniques required is the mental calm and clarity of thought needed to execute them.

1

To escape a bear hug with
arms pinned, slam
your attackers face
with your head.

2

Stomp his instep with
your heel.

3

Third, use your "C" step,
elbow strike and
bottomfist as before.

4

After, run from the scene
as fast as possible.

If your attacker is down, it does not mean he is out. If he continues his advances even after your technique, follow up with a stomp to the groin.

elbow strike and Bottomfist as before. No hold is inescapable. The ability to stay calm and assess a situation with a clear mind can be your most potent weapon.

Whenever you throw a strike you should let rip with a visceral scream. In Korean, this scream is called a *"Kiyoop"*. A loud scream can not only bring the attention of passersby-bye to your plight, it is also a way to scare your opponent, to increase the power of your techniques and bolster confidence. A good kiyoop will cause virtually any untrained opponent to freeze for a moment. You can use this time to launch your next strike. Many taekwondo students yell the word "Kiyoop!" when they strike. Others develop distinctive yells. Whatever you decide, be sure to belt out your scream as loud as you can.

Yell as loud as you can whenever you strike. This will increase the power of your technique, improve your confidence and cause your attacker to freeze up for a moment--time you can seize upon to land another blow.

Practicing on a regular basis with your peers will help you acquire the confidence and self-esteem needed to carry yourself--and to defend yourself--with confidence and the conviction that you are more capable than your assailant.

Another common defense with which you should be familiar is that against a *side headlock*. It is not uncommon for an attacker who wishes to inflict serious harm on his victim to hold her in a headlock. Time is of the essence in such a situation; you must react before your assailant has time to hurt you. If you wait, you risk letting him intensify his grip or get in one or more punches. Absorbing these could seriously jeopardize your chances of escape. Developing the ability to respond immediately can be gained only as the result of assiduous practice. Ideas can be fascinating, but in the practical world of self-defense, it is your ability to apply concepts in real-life situations that determines success.

You must practice all of your self-defense movements from both sides. There is no such thing as being "righty" or "lefty" in taekwondo. Let's assume

Escaping from a headlock might seem impossible, but it's not. However, you must react quickly and with certitude.

98

that your attacker has you in a *side headlock* with his right arm. To escape, step forward at a 45-degree angle with your right leg. Land in a stance that is twice as wide as your shoulders with your knees pointed outward, toward your toes, which should point straight ahead. As you do this, make fists and raise your arms. Slam them in concurrently, landing the Bottomfist of your right hand into your assailant's

There is no such thing as "lefty" or "righty" in taekwondo. You must be able to carry out any technique equally well on both sides.

groin and that of your left to his lower ribs. Now, reach up with your left hand and grab his hair (if he has none, reach your hand into his face and grab whatever you can). Pull his hair backward thus lifting and exposing his chin. Curl back the fingers of your right hand and slam your palm into his chin. Keep your right hand planted in his face and use the leverage to throw him over your left leg in a circular motion. There are essentially three movements to this technique: stepping out, slamming in your strikes, and then the throw. You must be able to throw one after the other smoothly and to begin with no hesitation.

Another grab from which you will need an escape is a *two handed choke*. To escape, interlock your hands as you step back with your right leg. Shoot your hands straight out into your attackers upper lip. Now reach your hands behind his head and pull him into a knee strike to the groin. Be sure to "Kiyoop!" as loud as you can when executing any strike.

Sometimes an assault may be indirect. If, for instance, someone were to grab your wrist to take

1

*First, step forward
and raise both hands.
in fists.*

2

*Second, strike the
groin and ribs
concomittantly.*

3

*Third, pull the hair back
and expose the
assailant's chin.*

4

*Fourth, slam in your
palm strike and use the
striking hand to send
your opponent reeling
over your left leg.*

101

If you are caught in a choke, don't wait. React immediately. Your options are never as limited as fear might have you believe .

102

If you are caught in a two handed choke, you must react immediately.

you somewhere against your will, it may seem as if you have no choice. This is not the case. Defending against wrist grabs is a relatively simple business for which there are many options. As one example, assume someone is grabbing your right wrist with their left hand. All you need do is wrap your hand around his left clockwise and step forward with your right leg. As you do this, place your body weight

Interlace you fingers as you step back

Then shoot your striking area into your opponent's upper lip.

103

on the upper part of his arm. Press on it firmly. Done properly, this will cause writhing pain and help your assailant understand the seriousness of your intentions. If he still doesn't get the message, retain your grasp and slam your left knee into his face. In the foregoing example, the attacker was grabbing your right hand with his left. If he was facing you, he was thus reaching forward, not across. If, however, he did a "cross-grab" and went for your right hand

with his right, you need to react a little differently. This time, wrap your hand around his forearm counter-clockwise and step your left leg in front of both of his legs. Exert pressure on his right arm in a downward *and circular* motion. Use this force to sweep your assailant's legs. As he falls,

Defending against a wrist grab is relatively simple-- if you react without hesitation.

retain your grasp on his arm and bend his right wrist with your right hand. Keep your left hand near his right elbow. If he does not have a believable change of heart, use this force to break his arm and wrist. Escape the scene as soon as possible. Always notify the police after any self-defense situation, whether you succeeded or not.

There are several effective counters to a wrist grab. You should try to familiarize yourself with as many as possible. Should one fail, you may then find recourse in another.

In a street encounter, you must use whatever force you deem necessary to protect yourself.

-7-
Sexual Harassment

T o prove a charge of sexual harrassment, according to a the Federal Court's ruling in the Mendey Vs. The US Air Force, one "must prove by preponderant evidence that alleged harrassment conduct occurred, that it was unwelcome to person to whom it was directed, that it was of sexual nature, and that it unreasonably interfered with individual's work performance or created an

As you think about sexual harassment, it is important that you associate specific types of behavior on the part of others with specific reactions on your part.

Although the courts have been hesitant to provide a clear legal definition of sexual harassment, you must be clear as to what--in your mind--constitutes sexual harassment

intimidating, hostile or offensive working environment through conduct sufficiently severe and persistent to affect seriously the psychological well-being of harrassed employee." Arguments also can be made that sexual harrassment is a violation of the Equal Protection Clause of the Constitution. In addition, Title VII of the Civil Rights Act of 1964 prohibits discrimination in the workplace because of sex. The turbulence surrounding the Clarence Thomas Supreme Court nomination has shed new light on the

1. <u>Mendey V Department of Air Force</u>, MSPB 1988 38 M.S.P.R. 659

fact that the courts have in fact been reluctant to provide a clearly defined answer to the question as to what, exactly, sexual harrassment is. However, it is clear that many incidents of sexual harrasment go unreported. Even before the much publicized Thomas nomination and the subsequent uproar over the allegations of his sexually harassing Professor Anita Hill, many studies had indicated that sexual harrassment was a widespread although rarely discussed problem. One survey, conducted by Claire

As many as nine out of ten women have experienced sexual harassment. Taekwondo practice will give you the confidence, skill and courage needed to prevent sexual harassment. Once you become proficient in taekwondo, your confidence outside the dojang will send a strong message to potential criminals.

Safran in the November 1976 issue of *Redbook Magazine*, found that, out of 9,000 women, nine of of 10 answered that they had been sexually harassed. In an article published in 1973 called "Absent from the Majority: Working Class Women in America," Nancy Seifer found that 81 percent of the women surveyed in a naval base and a nearby town reported some form of sexual harrassment. It is not unusual that women had not risen up against a crime which, until the Thomas hearings, really had no name. However, problems related to the lack of public awareness, a dearth of information and the subsequent lack of concern are compounded by the fact that targets of sexual harrassment are not selected at random. Women who are shy, easily embarrassed or intimidated are easy prey for employers, co-workers or others who feel obliged to embarrass, insult, touch, or otherwise harass them. Passifism and complacency are common reactions among women who are fearful of reporting the crime.

If you train regularly you will feel better about yourself and thus be less inclined to let anyone change that perception.

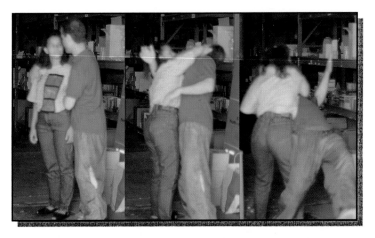

The typical scenario is that of older men harassing younger women to whom the women feel no attraction. Remember, sexual harassment takes many forms. If someone is doing something that makes you feel uncomfortable, put an immediate halt to it. Silence can easily be misconstrued as acceptance.

Despite the public clamor that followed the Thomas hearing, the point was made during and after the questioning of Professor Hill that sexual harrassment is not the sort of problem most women discuss readily. Thus the inference should not be made that a charge of sexual harrassment can now be made without the victim feeling the risk of stigmatization. The typical scenario seems to be that of young women harrassed by older men by whom they are employed and would never choose as sexual partners. However, the legal amiguities and societal confusion have only passing relevance to the taekwondo practitioner. People who live in accord with taekwondo philosophy do not need an interpretive legal analysis to determine how to react. Often, people allow their intuitive abilities to be squelched because they are fearful of retribution, defeat or the loss of a job. As your confidence increases, you will not only find that your instincts become more refined, but that your ability to speak up and articulate your feelings does as well. A taekwondo practitioner thus puts sexual harrassment in a broader

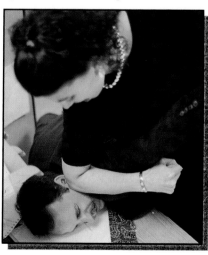

People who live in accordance with taekwondo's philosophy have little patience for those who seek to humiliate, degrade or otherwise harm them.

The attitudinal changes that occur as a result of your taekwondo training are always active. Taekwondo practitioners are taught to respect others, but they must also respect themselves. Being able to handle a situation involving sexual harassment will be relatively easy after a few months of formal training.

context, i.e., she reacts to lude remarks, insinuations, threats and physical harrassment in the workplace the same as she would outside it. Taekwondo students strive to acquire focused, clear minds and strong, physically sound bodies. These characteristics do not fluctuate during "off hours," and it is thus the responsibility of any taekwondo student to deal with sexual harrassment with force commensurate to the degree of discomfort or danger posed.

Much of what you learn in the physical aspect of

Learning to react as your opponent is himself attacking is an important part of the physical aspect of taekwondo. It is also a trait that will carry over into your life outside the dojang and will help you cut off an attack before it can harm you.

taekwondo spills over into the mental. For instance, when you spar and feel your opponent is about to launch a blow, you must react first, striking him before he has the chance. Moreover, the fact that he is trying to strike you often works to your advantage. You can combine his incoming force with that of your outgoing momentum to create substantial impact. This notion--of striking first with a formidable blow that undermines your attacker's impending assault--is relevant to anyone who gives thought to what sexual harassment is. Although the laws may be ambiguous, you must have a clearly defined notion as to what the issue means to you and to react in a way you consider appropriate. Your training in taekwondo will greatly expand the options at your disposal. Your increased confidence, self-esteem and the fact that you can back up harsh words with force will be factors working to your advantage. To react to sexual harrassment effectively, you must use the same concept as the

It is important that you be able to back-up harsh words. However, if you feel your safety or well-being is at stake, strike first and hard. To wait for an opponent to strike so your maneuver can be deemed "defensive" is dangerous and foolhardy.

taekwondo practitioner who reacts against his opponent's assault as it is underway. *The first time* someone in the workplace makes remarks with which you are uncomfortable, you should interrupt him in as stern a manner as possible, telling him in no uncertain terms that he is sexually harrassing you. Put your complaint into a formal letter. Distribute it to his supervisor, the personnel office, that of the company president and every executive in the company. Many companies have recently adopted new policies to

If you wish, you may warn the person who is harassing you. If you choose to do so, do it the first time it occurs and advise as many people as possible about the situation, in the office and outside it.

deter sexual harrassment. Whether your's has one or not, make your uneasiness known the moment you feel it happening or even beginning to happen. Remember, silence is easily misconstrued as acceptance.

Sexual harassment takes many forms; it can be verbal or physical. Verbal sexual harrassment can include passing remarks on a woman's body to *Redbook's* description of an eighteen year old girl

Bear in mind: Sexual harassment takes many forms from verbal innuendos to outright rape. Do not let any form of sexual harassment take you buy surprise.

whose supervisor would regularly call her into his office "to tell me the intimate details of his marriage." Physical forms of sexual harrassment range from a pinch to outright molestation and rape. One woman in the *Redbook* survey said her supervisor "runs his hand up my leg or blouse. He hugs me to him and then tells me that he is 'just naturally affectionate.'" Despite the obvious impropriety, many women are fearful of warding off such "natural affections." As Catherine MacKinnon notes on page 35 of her groundbreaking book *Sexual Harrassment of Working Women:* "Sudden allegations of job incompetence and poor attitude commonly follow rejection of sexual advances and are used to support employment consequences." If you are not training in taekwondo, flee the scene once you feel uncomfortable and report the incident immediately. If you are training, your response to an unwelcome physical advance must also be physical. If, for instance, someone puts his arm around you in an unwelcome hug, act receptive, return his embrace and suggest that you would like to go for a walk. Then, as you stroll arm in arm (assume you are on the left), sweep out his right leg the second before his step touches ground. This will plant him on the floor and cause back and/or head injuries. You should then immediately report the incident and explain that you refuse to let an incident of sexual harrassment occur before acting against it. You can prevent sexual harrassment, whether it's verbal or physical. To do so, you must define to yourself what situations make you feel uncomfortable. Then, you must decide what reaction is appropriate for each scenerio. With training in taekwondo, you will have the capacity to immediately end such situations. It will help you refine your instincts and give you the confidence you need to act in a way that does not run counter to them.

-8-
The Basic Rules of Safety

We have talked thus far about what to do if you're attacked. How to avoid a confrontation altogether is another question, which anyone concerned with self-defense and basic safety issues must address. The way in which you talk, walk, act and behave in general has much to do with whether you will be targeted as a victim of

Making eye contact can serve notice that you have no intention of complying with a potential assailant's wishes.

The majority of rape victims know the rapist. It is therefore essential that you send a message of confidence when speaking with acquaintances. Going out in groups is also a useful preventative measure you may wish to take until an acquaintance has earned your trust.

violent crime. No one "asks" to be such a victim. Nevertheless, the way in which one conducts herself when faced with a potential attacker may be enough to deter the assault. *Eye contact,* for instance, can signal a disagreeable sense of assertiveness to a potential rapist or mugger. Statistics suggest that many rapists were at some point acquainted with their victims. If, for instance, an acquaintance makes a remark you consider rude, offensive or indicative of aggressive behavior, maintain eye contact and address the issue on the spot. Tell the person, without waiting to see if it was a "slip," that you found the remark distasteful. Remember, criminals and potential criminals have a lot on the line. If they choose the wrong person, they could end up hurt, killed or imprisoned. Be sure to convey the message that you are a confident person, able to stand up for and defend yourself.

If an acquaintance makes a remark you consider rude, uncalled for or vulgar, speak up and cut him off right away. Do not let it "slip by."

While only you can decide what lifestyle suits you best, certain ways of behaving, such as going out at night alone, has been correlated with incidences of rape and other violent crimes.

There is much to be said about trusting your instincts. If, for instance, someone is saying or doing something that feels wrong, it probably is. Again, confidence is they key word.

Your general lifestyle has an obvious effect on the degree of danger you are likely to encounter. If you are in the habit of going out unaccompanied with people you do not know well, of frequenting night clubs alone, drinking excessively or using other

Drinking, especially when you're alone with people you do not know, has been shown to increase the risk of crimes such as rape. By drinking, you decrease your general awareness, increase your susceptibility to danger from those around you who become less inhibited and impair coordination, which is needed in taking control of a self-defense situation.

intoxicants, you increase the likelihood of encountering a situation in which your safety is jeopardized.

Your *driving habits* also affect the degree of danger to which you are exposed. If you frequently drive in wooded areas, in areas with poor lighting, reduced visibility or limited phone access, the potential for danger increases. Sometimes simple acts of prevention go unaddressed. For instance, you should always have jumper cables in your trunk and know how to use them. A white cloth or towel can be useful in signalling for help. Hanging it outside your window when your car is stopped indicates that you need assistance. Also, never drive with less than a quarter of a tank of gas. Check your tire pressure on a regular basis. Have a usable spare in the trunk and

Your driving habits can seriously influence the likelihood of attack. If at all possible , avoid driving alone. Also, learn to change a spare and to use jumper cables.

Learning control, of yourself, those around you and of your environment is an essential part of your taekwondo training.

Try to avoid driving in heavily wooded areas where help is hard to find. If you must do so on a regular basis, you may find a car phone to be a worthy investment.

know how to put it on. If you've been having car trouble, avoid using the car altogether until it is fixed. Locking your car is one of the easiest and most effective deterrents to crime. It is also one of the most neglected. When you return to a parking lot, you should always look inside to be sure there is no intruder in the back seat. Carrying a flashlight when you go out at night--several types fit easily into a purse--is one way to do this more effectively. If you do find someone in your car, do not confront him. Run as far from the scene as possible and notify the police. When you are in a busy parking lot, it is best to park as close to the store as you can. More importantly, take note of what is taking place. As you walk from your car to a store entrance, get into the habit of "people watching." Time and again it is said by victims of violent crime that they saw their assailant and had an "eery feeling." Your instincts are vital for your protection, Learn to refine and trust

Carrying a flashlight when you leave your car (many fit easily into your purse) can be helpful in checking your car before re-entering it, which you should always do.

129

them. If you are preoccupied with the things you must buy as you approach a store, your imperviousness to your surroundings will be evident from your outward appearance. Muggers, rapists and like-minded people look for this. By conditioning yourself to observe--not just see--your surroundings, you will be more apt to react appropriately should danger present itself. Although expensive, a *car*

Your instincts and powers of observation can be vital assets in both preventing and defending against violent attacks. When in a parking lot, for instance, be in the habit of asking yourself: "Should this person be where he is?"

Muggers and other thugs are on the look-out for people who seem preoccupied with their thoughts and thus somewhat oblivious to their surroundings. Staying aware of your surroundings does not mean you are paranoid. It indicates that you are taking intelligent steps to protect yourself. Here, one gets the impression of a woman who is well aware of what is going on around her.

phone is a handy item which can help you elude danger. If you are trapped in your car or witnessing a crime, a car-phone may prove a worthy investment.

Your powers of observation can be refined so as to help you prevent trouble before it begins. Bear in mind that not all muggers look the role. You must always ask yourself: "Does this person belong here?"

If you are accustomed to seeing certain people in the hallways as you leave work at night but today you see a new person standing idle, assume the worst. It may well be that he is waiting for someone, that he has some business in the area or that he is simply relaxing. But there are ways to determine just how much someone seems out of place. If you're in a parking lot in sweltering heat and a man is following you in heavy clothing, head for the entrance or back to the car, whichever is closer. If you have a car phone, or when

If someone seems out of place, assume he is.

132

you get to the pay phone in the mall, call the police. If you are not sure whether to call, do it and have no fear about being embarrassed. The police will understand. But remember that you can always be of better assistance when you can provide them with a detailed description of the potential assailant. Observe the behavior of the people around you as well as their location and dress. Can you get to safety before the

If someone is following you when in the car, do not drive home. Go to the nearest police station and do your best to get a description of the car and person.

stranger near you attacks? If so, remember that seemingly innocent suggestions and questions such as "Hold up!" "Do you have change?" or "Do you know the time?" can all be ploys meant to entice you into an assailant's trap. Stay on the move. Many incidents begin with non-threatening questions then rely on the element of surprise. When you learn to isolate danger and react accordingly, you are taking a step toward avoiding harm. If you are assaulted, your main

Seemingly innocent questions, such as "Do you have the time?" can be an assailant's trap to close the distance between you and him. If you do answer the question, do not close the distance between the two of you. You should in fact try to increase it.

Women are raped and assaulted every day because they did not prepare for an attack. Remember, most attackers have a plan. You must have a better plan. Training in taekwondo is the best preparation possible.

objective is to survive. Women are raped and killed every year because they failed to prepare for danger. Remember, a criminal is probably someone with a plan. He has probably thought about his crime, advanced to a confrontational stage and is committed to carrying it out. Rarely does a criminal change his mind mid-way through an attack. You must be more

A rapist or mugger is someone who has made a commitment--rarely will either change his mind midway through an attack. Your commitment, to your training and your protection, must be greater than his. You must therefore train on a regular basis to refine the skills you need. If you do this, you will find that your skills actually exceed the demands of such situations. Escape will then be relatively easy.

committed than he, in terms of your efforts to avoid a confrontation and in your determination to not only survive it but to do so with ease. If you train regularly, you will not panic. Your clarity of thought and defensive abilities will confound the average attacker. It is o.k. to be scared. It is not o.k. to lose control. If you fail in a self-defense maneuver, don't panic. Try it again with an eye for the best alternative--one always exists. You can survive virtually any unarmed assault. But it takes hard work, in a taekwondo school and outside it as well. If you prepare now, you'll be ready should the time come.

One scenario that replays itself daily on city streets is that of a woman having her purse snatched. What should you do if someone tries to grab your

Learning discipline and patience are essential parts of your taekwondo training that will carry over into life outside the taekwondo school and help you to carry out your self-defense techniques with total commitment.

purse? If you are not training in taekwondo, the answer is to simply let go Without training, you'll be risking too much by putting up a fight you can't back up. Let it go. If you are training, let go only if you see or believe the assailant has a weapon. Otherwise, fight back. When he grabs it, wrap your arm around your purse-string, thrust a sidekick into the side of his knee and land forward with a forearm to his temple. If you need to, follow up with an elbow from the opposite direction or with any of the other strikes

If you are untrained in taekwondo and someone tries to steal your purse, let it go. It is not worth risking harm and the chances of defeating your attacker are slim.

138

If you are training regularly in taekwondo, you will see that you need not relinquish your purse. There are several techniques designed for just such situations, and if your attacker is unarmed, you should have no hesitation in using them. Remember, however, that determining whether a mugger is armed or unarmed can itself be in a risky, if not deadly business. You must be as certain as the circumstances and reason allow.

you've learned. By training in taekwondo, you will have the ability to easily outclass the average assailant. You should do everything you can to avoid a confrontation. When one does arise, though, you must ensure that it is you who walks away unharmed.

Another scenario you may encounter is that of being followed. If you suspect you are being followed, do not go home, although this might feel natural. You do not want this person to know where you live. Try to re-route yourself to a busy area. Constantly check to see if he is still there. If he is, go

It is essential that you let rip with your strike as soon as possible when performing this technique. If you wrap your arm but hesitate before striking, this gives the assailant time to free himself up to harm you.

If you suspect someone is following you on the street, do not go home. You do not want this person to know where you live. Try to get to as busy an area as possible, or a police station. If he does get a hold of you, you must react with your techniques immediately. Hesitating can prove costly.

to the nearest police station and explain. They will usually not be able to make an arrest based on his following you. But they should be able to identify and talk to him, and they may be able to make an arrest for previously served warrants.

With proper instruction, you can greatly reduce the risk of rape or assault. If you are raped, however, do not bathe or shower. Call the police immediately. Nationwide, only one out of 15 rapes is reported. The fear of reporting rape has let far too many criminals roam free and decreases rapists' fear of carrying out the crime against other women.

-9-
Taekwondo as an Art and Way of Life

While the techniques you have read about heretofore emphasize how taekwondo techniques may be used in a self-defense situation, it would be misleading to imply that taekwondo is merely a system of self-defense. In fact, taekwondo is rooted in 2000 years of history, having been called at various times *Tae Kyon, Soobak* and

Taekwondo is much more than a means of self-defense. It is an ancient art with a rich heritage .

143

Statue of Warrior 'Kumgang , in Sokkuram cave in Kyungju (7th Century)

Archaeologists have discovered drawings in an ancient royal tomb in Korea, called the Muyong Chong, which suggest taekwondo is at least 2000 years old.

Tang Soo Do. Evidence of taekwondo's early existence was found in the *Muyong Chong,* a royal tomb in Korea. When archaeologists unearthed this tomb, they discovered pictures of people practicing movements very similar to those practiced by taekwondo students today. As taekwondo developed through the years, discord among the various schools or *kwans* prevented the taekwondo community from

144

unifying. Today, however, *The World Taekwondo Federation (WTF)* is the undisputed governing body, sanctioning all taekwondo competitions and certifying all belt promotions at the black belt level and above.

Many practitioners feel that the artistic side of taekwondo is best represented by its forms or *poomse*. Forms are pre-arranged patterns of taekwondo movements. Each movement represents that technique's ideal execution, and the practice of

Taekwondo forms or "poomse" are one representation of the artistic side of taekwondo. The movements in a form are said to represent their ideal execution, and practitioners constantly seek to improve themselves by improving their forms.

Taekwondo practitioners must adhere to strict ethical guidelines. These are constantly reinforced in the taekwondo school and greatly influence the life of anyone who practices the art. Respect is one of the most important things you will learn in taekwondo. One way taekwondo practitioners express respect is by bowing.

forms is thus considered one way in which taekwondo practitioners strive toward mental and physical perfection. Above all, however, taekwondo students embrace the philosophical and ethical stipulations upon which the art is based; these come to define clear guidelines for their lives. As an

Taekwondo students must learn to help others as much as themselves. Working on techniques that require cooperation by both people is one way in which this gets reinforced.

example, taekwondo practitioners strive toward five goals: *Respect, Humility, Perseverance, Self-Control* and *Honesty.* In addition, they must adhere to eleven commandments: *Loyalty to your country, Respect your Parents, Faithfulness to your Spouse, Respect your Brothers and Sisters, Loyalty to your Friends, Respect Your Teachers, Respect Your Elders, Never Take Life Unjustly, Have an Indomitable Spirit,*

147

Finish What You Begin and *Loyalty to Your School.* While they may seem insignificant in and of themselves, the constant drive to personify these ethical guidelines is a challenge from which hundreds of thousands of taekwondo students have reaped great reward. You may wonder why anyone concerned with self-defense need even spend time pondering such seemingly remote ideas. The reason is that they are far from remote. A taekwondo

The strict rules of the dojang help students develop a sense of respect and discipline.

practitioner's goal is never to simply be proficient in self-defense--this can be accomplished in a matter of months. However, proficiency in taekwondo takes several years, and the earning of a black belt, after about three or fours years, is typically thought to be just the beginning of a lifelong journey. As you become more adept in forms practice, you will find yourself continually setting higher goals for yourself, in the taekwondo school and out. Once you reach

Taekwondo students are constantly setting new, higher goals for themselves.

Meditation or "Chung Shin Tomil" is another essential part of your taekwondo training. Meditating will help you develop the clarity of mind needed to make decisions and react in ways with which you feel comfortable.

them, you will feel satisfaction, but you will nevertheless have already set an even higher goal. One's study of taekwondo is thus never completed as one can never truly satisfy herself that she has reached her fullest potential.

Another way in which taekwondo practitioners strive to improve themselves is by meditation or *"Chung Shin Tomil."* Before and after any taekwondo

Students meditate before and after every taekwondo class, first to clear their minds from thoughts that might distract them from training. Meditation also helps students to visualize and actualize their goals.

class, the students meditate. During this time you may do one of two things. First, you may be asked to clear your mind of all thought and to relax completely. You will find this easier after a rigorous training session. This method of meditating is also useful before beginning physical exercise because it helps rid the mind of diversionary thought and to thereby prepare for serious practice. It is impossible to practice taekwondo while being concerned about work worries or other extraneous thought. Once you can meditate this way, you will perform your taekwondo movements with an uncommon clarity of thought. You will also discover that this type of thinking need not be limited to practice time. As you work, interact with family and friends or pursue any of your personal interests, you will find that the mental/attitudinal benefits of taekwondo training are a guiding force in

Meditation is useful to you in many respects: It helps you to relax, focus your thoughts, isolate your goals and develop a positive, winning attitude that will help you achieve them.

your life. The second method of meditation is related to visualization. During this time, your *sabumnim* will ask that you first achieve a state of relaxation. He will then ask that you visualize yourself achieving a new goal. For some students it is the perfect execution of a kick. For others, it is achieving the flexibility required to do a split. Others seek complete mastery

Your taekwondo master or "sabumnim" will be there to guide you through every stage of your development in taekwondo. Many students find that they develop a special relationship with their sabumnim in that he helps them to dig deep and pull out their very best. He is also often regarded as a friend, mentor and confidant who takes pride in his students mental and physical achievements.

Breaking or "kyuk Pah" is one way in which you may measure the increased power you develop as you become more advanced in taekwondo.

of themselves. During this time of visualization, the latter students see themselves as complete masters of their bodies and minds. People occasionally get caught up in the hustle and bustle of daily life and forget their true goals. When you can better isolate them, it is easier to actualize them. Many students whose time is consumed by work visualize themselves having improved relationships with their family and/or friends. This is far from an unattainable goal, and

154

most students find that this technique, combined with the confidence and self-esteem they have acquired from training, is of great importance in realizing and focusing on those goals to which they truly aspire. Although you will find yourself improving in your forms and achieving greater clarity of thought by meditating, you will invariably find the physical benefits of taekwondo rewarding as well. Increased

Improved relationships, better work habits, organizational skills and patience are just some of the qualities you will develop and refine in your training. Taekwondo is easily the best means of self-defense available. It is also a way of life-- and a way of improving life.

Sparring practice is a safe and effective way of learning timing, increasing your speed and agility and improving your confidence. While it may seem frightening at first, you will find sparring to be an enjoyable way of testing out new techniques, and of testing yourself. All students who participate in sparring classes are required to wear full safety gear.

endurance, flexibility, strength, a more efficient immune system and a sound cardiovascular system: all will result from earnest training. These too will manifest outside the dojang. Tasks that had previously required great exertion will feel easy. You will have an energetic, enthusiastic and positive attitude and you will come to regard yourself as a uniquely talented and capable person. All of these assets will help you develop confidence, self-esteem and an irrepressible desire to achieve as much as you can, in the dojang and out. Many people begin their study of taekwondo to learn self-defense. They usually stay, however, for much loftier reasons. Taekwondo offers an approach to life that highlights a positive mental and physical approach. The study of taekwondo is a lifelong venture, and the rewards of its practice are plentiful. Only you can make the decision to improve yourself with taekwondo. Of one thing you can be sure: When you do begin, the rewards will far exceed the demands. The most important step is the first. And that is simply getting started. When you take it, you will be taking a big step in learning self-defense, and in discovering your true potential, physically, mentally, and spiritually.

Glossary

Ahp Chagi
Front Snap Kick

Nerie Chagi
Axe Kick

Chumuck Chirugi
Backfist

Palgup Chigi
Forearm Strike

Chumuck
Fist

Poomse
Form

Chung Shin Tomil
Meditation

Sabumnim
Master

Dojang
Taekwondo School

Taekwondo
Foot, Hand, Way of
Life

Dolryo Chagi
Roundhouse Kick

**Tae Kyon, Soobak,
Tang Soo Do**
Old Names for
Taekwondo

Kiyoop
Yell

Kyroogi Sparring

Twi Chumuck
Reverse Punch

Kyroogi Jay Say
Fighting Stance

Yop Chagi
Side Kick

Muyong Chong
Royal Tomb in Korea

Index